1B

COME PLAY WITH ME

Modern Curriculum Press
BEGINNING
TO
READ
Series

COME PLAY WITH ME

Margaret Hillert

Illustrated by Kinuko Craft

MODERN CURRICULUM PRESS
Cleveland • Toronto

ISBN 0-8136-5036-4 Hardcover
ISBN 0-8136-5536-6 Paperback

Library of Congress Catalog Card Number: 75-884

1 2 3 4 5 6 7 8 9 10   99 98 97 96 95 94 93

COME PLAY WITH ME

My Dog and I

My dog can jump.

My dog can jump.

My dog can play and run.

And I can jump.

I like to jump.

My dog and I have fun.

7

My Playhouse

I have a little playhouse—
Yellow, red, and blue.
I like it in my playhouse,
And you will like it, too.

8

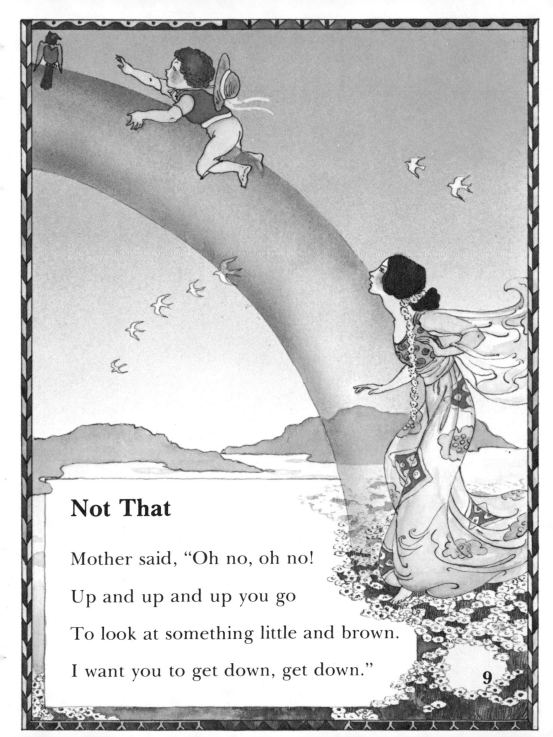

Not That

Mother said, "Oh no, oh no!

Up and up and up you go

To look at something little and brown.

I want you to get down, get down."

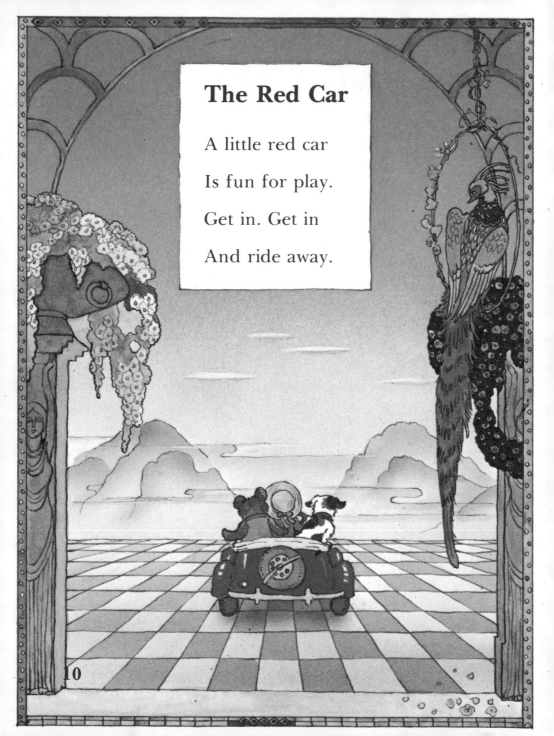

The Red Car

A little red car

Is fun for play.

Get in. Get in

And ride away.

10

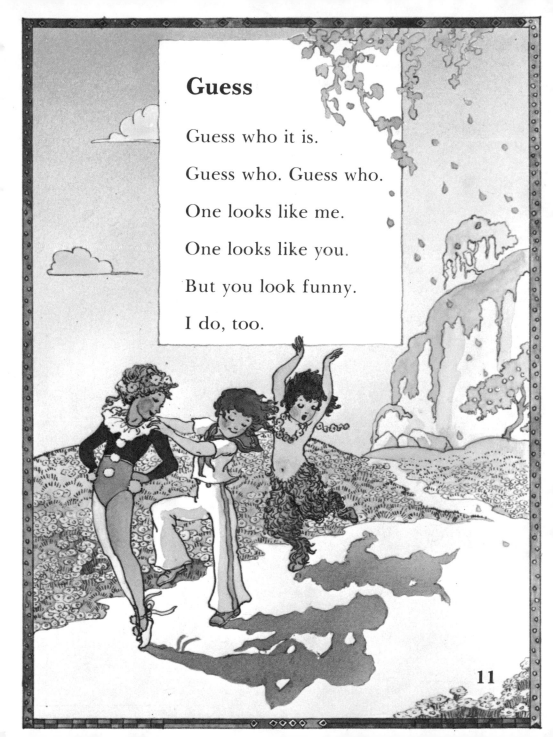

Guess

Guess who it is.

Guess who. Guess who.

One looks like me.

One looks like you.

But you look funny.

I do, too.

11

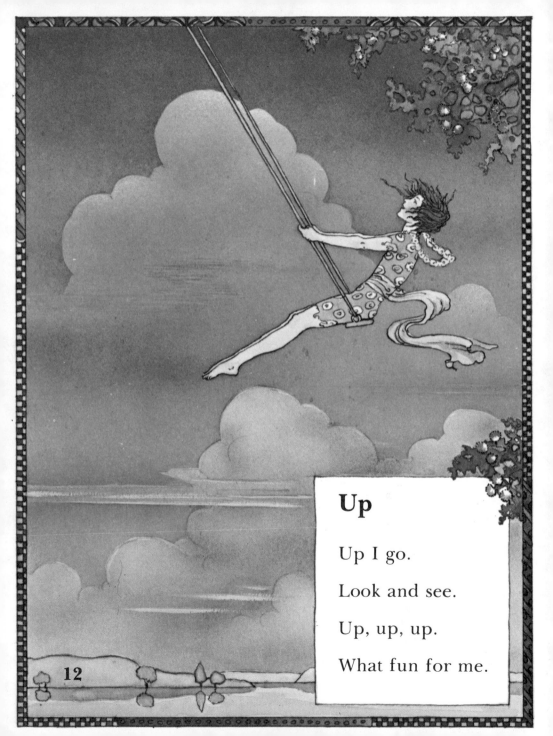

Up

Up I go.

Look and see.

Up, up, up.

What fun for me.

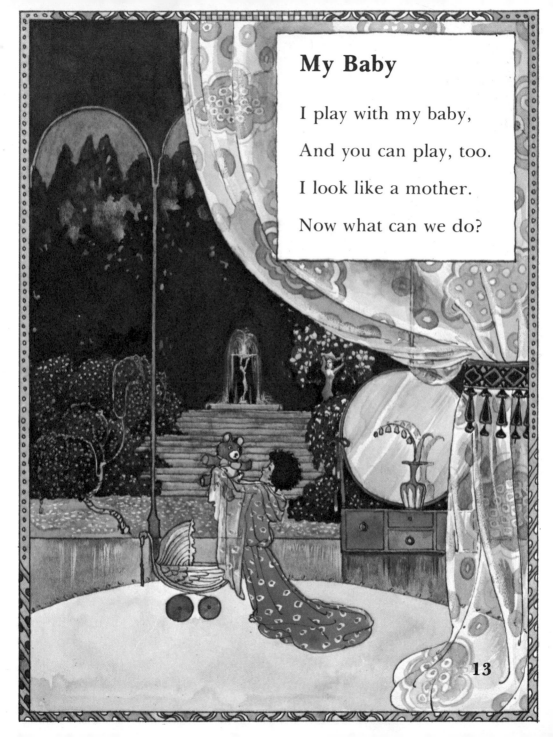

My Baby

I play with my baby,

And you can play, too.

I look like a mother.

Now what can we do?

13

A Ball

Up and down.

Up and down.

A ball can go up.

A ball can come down.

Fun with Father

Father, Father,

Run, run, run.

I like to play with you.

What fun.

15

My Book

I like to look

In a book, book, book

To see what I can see.

A book is fun.

Now you get one

And see what you can see.

16

The Boat

Oh, oh, oh.

The boat can go.

Go, go, go.

Little boat, go.

17

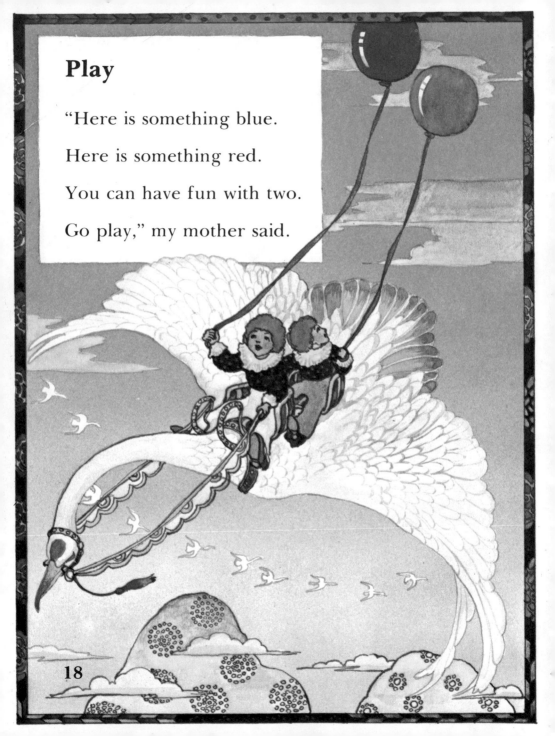

Play

"Here is something blue.

Here is something red.

You can have fun with two.

Go play," my mother said.

18

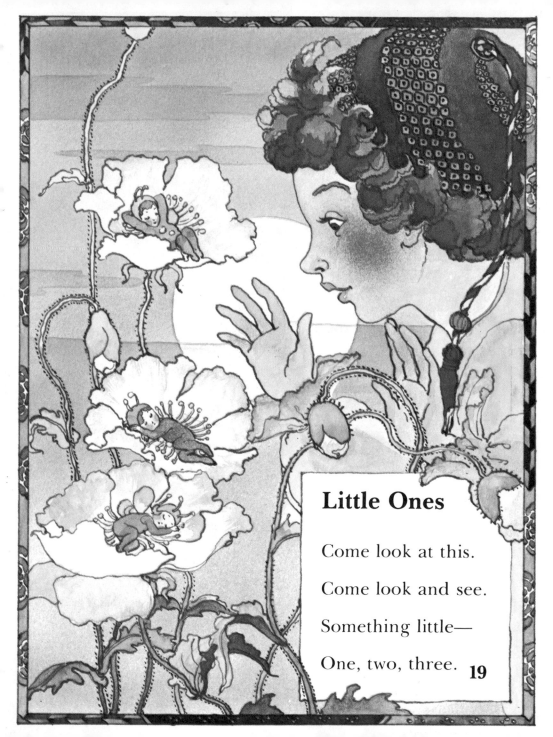

Little Ones

Come look at this.

Come look and see.

Something little—

One, two, three. **19**

Work

I like to help my mother work.

My mother likes it, too.

I like to help my father work.

Here's something I can do.

20

Jump

Jump a little.

Jump a little.

One, two, three.

Jump a little.

Jump a little.

Play with me.

21

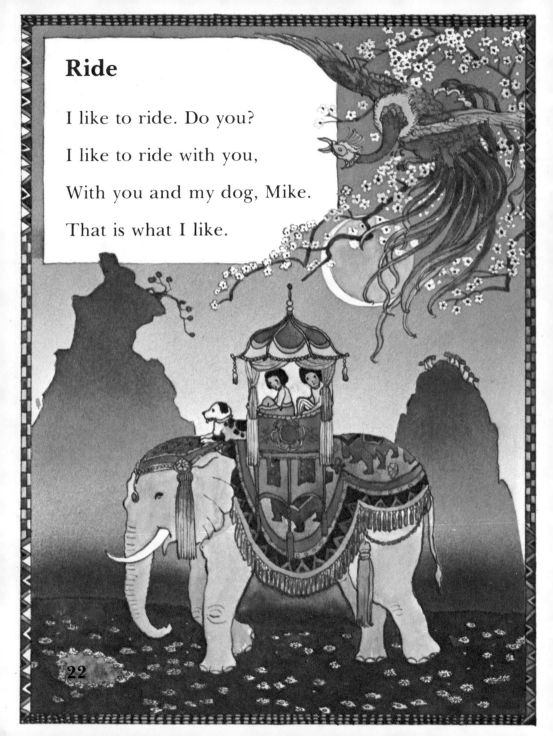

Ride

I like to ride. Do you?

I like to ride with you,

With you and my dog, Mike.

That is what I like.

22

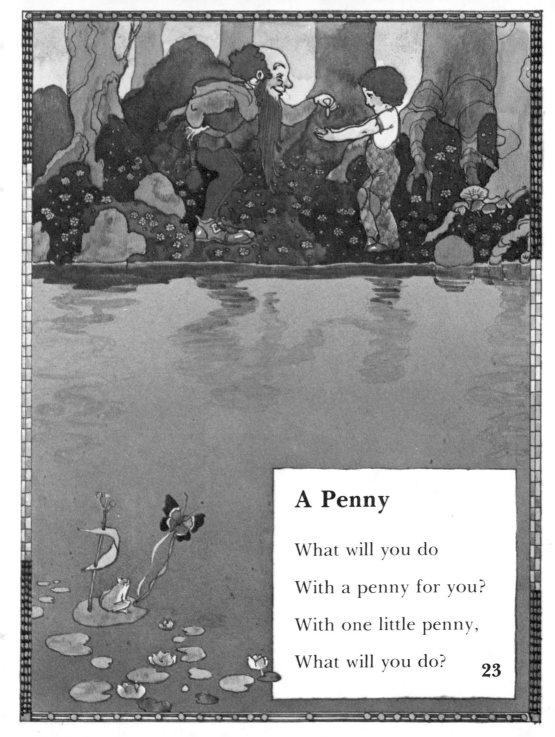

A Penny

What will you do

With a penny for you?

With one little penny,

What will you do? **23**

Jump In

Oh, my. Oh, my.

I guess that I

Will jump in here

And play. Oh, my.

24

Look for Me

One, two, three.

Come look for me.

Did you find my spot?

No, you did not.

25

Cookies

My mother said to help.

Now see what we can do

With cookies, cookies, cookies

For me and you and you.

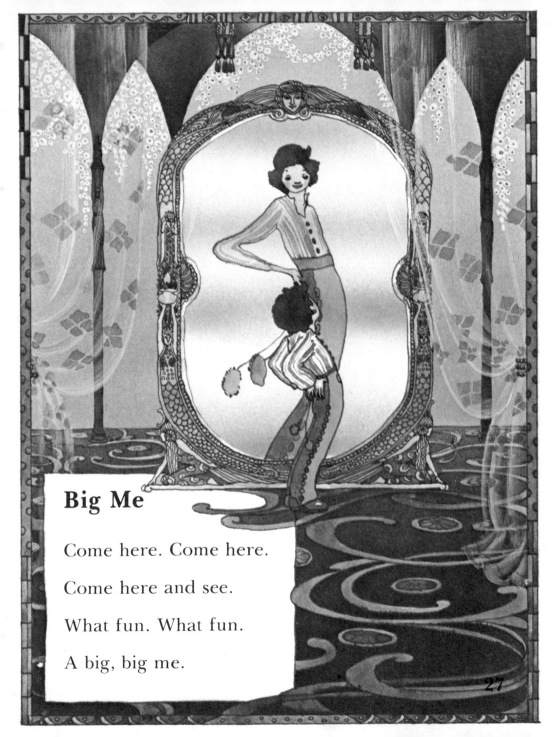

Big Me

Come here. Come here.

Come here and see.

What fun. What fun.

A big, big me.

Modern Curriculum Press Beginning-To-Read Books

Come Play with Me

Twenty-one rhymes with charming illustrations provide an introduction to verse for the youngest readers. The verses employ a vocabulary of 75 preprimer words.

Word List

7 my	mother	do
dog	said	**12** see
and	oh	what
I	no	**13** baby
can	up	with
jump	go	now
play	look(s)	we
run	at	**14** ball
like(s)	something	come
to	brown	**15** father
have	want	**16** book
fun	get	**17** boat
8 playhouse	down	**18** here
a	**10** the	two
little	car	**19** this
yellow	is	three
red	for	**20** work
blue	ride	help
it	away	**22** Mike
in	**11** guess	**23** penny
you	who	**25** did
will	one(s)	find
too	me	spot
9 not	but	**26** cookies
that	funny	**27** big

Uses of These Books. These books are planned for the very youngest readers, those who have been learning to read for about six to eight weeks and who have a small preprimer reading vocabulary. The books are written by Margaret Hillert, a first-grade teacher in the Royal Oak, Michigan, schools. Each book is illustrated in full color.

Because of their high interest and readability, these books are ideal for independent reading by primary and pre-primary children—at school, in the library, and at home. The books may also be incorporated into the basic reading program to develop children's interests, expand their vocabularies, and improve word-attack skills. It has been suggested that they might serve as the foundation for a skillfully directed reading program.

Careful attention is given to vocabulary load and sentence length, but the first criterion is interest to children. They will read *JUST Beginning-To-Read* books with confidence, with success, and with real enjoyment.